Where Did Christmas Come From?

Foothills Congregational Church

Where Did Christmas Come From?

Al Remson

A Perigee Book

A Perigee Book
Published by The Berkley Publishing Group
200 Madison Avenue
New York, NY 10016

Book design by Richard Oriolo
Cover design by James R. Harris
Cover illustration by Betsy Franco Feeney

First edition: December 1996

Published simultaneously in Canada.

The Putnam Berkley World Wide Web site address is
http://www.berkley.com/berkley

LIBRARY OF CONGRESS CATALOGING-IN-PUBLICATION DATA
Remson, Al.
Where did Christmas come from? / Al Remson.—1st ed.
p. cm.
"A Perigee book."
Includes bibliographical references.
ISBN 0-399-52247-6
1. Christmas I. Title.
GT4985.R45 1996
394.2'663—dc20   96-7821
CIP

Printed in the United States of America

10   9   8   7   6   5   4   3   2   1

For

Alverne

The Loveliest Christmas Gift of All

Contents

Where Did Christmas Come From?

Where Did Christmas Come From?

Whether you open presents on Christmas Eve or Christmas Day, the setting is likely to have some of the traditional elements associated with Christmas.

Stockings "hung by the chimney with care."

A Yule log burning brightly.

Santas and sleigh bells on cards displayed around the room.

The tree glowing with colored lights and shiny ornaments.

You and your family around the tree opening gifts.

Carols playing on the radio.

At some time on Christmas Day, you will probably sit down to an elaborate feast.

It is a time of warm family feelings and great merriment.

Could there be a more traditional way to celebrate Christmas?

It's traditional now, but none of these practices are reported in the Bible. None were practiced at the time of the birth of Christ. Who is Santa Claus? How did these traditions begin? Why do we celebrate Christmas in this way?

Where did Christmas —*Christmas as we know it*—come from?

Christmas Day

It's Christmas! The day that Jesus was born. Or is it? No one knows exactly on which day He was born. There is no official record of His birth. The evangelists, who wrote at least seventy years after Christ's death, left us a record of His teachings, but did not mention His birth date.

For three hundred years after His death, Christians celebrated His birthday on a variety of dates. Today, as in years past, the Russian Orthodox Christian church continues to celebrate Christmas on January 7.

Does it really matter on which date Jesus was born? Isn't His message more important? Before Jesus, there is no record of anyone preaching that we should love our enemies. This message was so central to His teaching and so unique that He thought it required an addition to the Ten Commandments! John reports Jesus as saying:

> *A new commandment I give unto you,*
> *That ye love one another.*

Christmas is a celebration of Jesus' message of love—the key theme of His ministry. But how did we come to celebrate His birth on December 25th?

December 25th

ometime close to the year A.D. 350, Pope Julius proclaimed December 25th as the date of the Nativity. How he chose the 25th is the result of influences from two very unlikely sources: pagan practices and military conquests.

In the old Roman calendar, December 25th was the shortest day of the year. From that date on, the sun would renew itself and burn longer each day until midsummer. To those who studied the sky for clues to the whims of the pagan gods, December 25th was sacred. It was a day of mystery and prophecy.

It was a date that was especially important to the Roman army. When they had conquered the lands of the Persians, the army had been exposed to a religion called Mithraism. Mithra, the Persian god of light, had been born on December 25th. The day the light began to renew itself was the signal for Mithra's birthday celebration. For reasons lost to antiquity, this religion quickly converted huge numbers of Roman

soldiers. Because most emperors came from army backgrounds, it was only natural for this Persian religion to eventually appear in Rome. The Romans recognized many religions and eventually gave Mithraism official status as a state religion.

Many other pagan religions had a celebration on or around December 25th. Yule was a Norse festival, lasting twelve days, in which log fires were kept burning to revive the fading sun (the source of our present-day Yule log). Rome celebrated Natalis Solis Invicti: the Feast of Lights—or Birthday of the Unconquered Sun.

One can find similar myths among South American Indians, ancient Celtic Druids, Persians, Orientals and Africans. Virtually all of these myths involve the renewal of the light, the rebirth of the sun, and have fire or some sort of glow as the centerpiece of their celebration.

The celebration of the renewal of the light must have spoken to a very deep-seated human need. These peoples wanted to be reassured that the depressing darkness would go away and that the gods would take care of them once more. With the return of the light they could look forward to the coming year with hope. They would gather together to celebrate with relief and great joy.

The return of the light, the glow of the hearth, the reassurance that the great supernatural powers would be kind and caring, and the joyousness that comes when the sun returns are the themes that would remain central to the winter celebration until our present day. No matter what else we celebrate, these themes are still reflected in our decorations, our songs and how we celebrate the holiday.

Pope Julius knew that Jesus was the light of the world. What better date on which to set his birthday than the date on which all could observe that the light had begun its return to mankind?

Two Holiday Traditions

By placing the celebration of Jesus' birth on December 25th, Pope Julius may have inadvertently left the church with a new set of problems. He probably hoped to provide Christians with an alternative to the lively and gaudy pagan celebrations. By A.D. 350 these ancient celebrations had lost much of their original religious significance and had become folk traditions. As Christianity spread, new converts simply added the Christian ways to celebrate Jesus' message of love to their old folk celebrations.

Over hundreds of years the two ways to celebrate blended together. As time went on conservative church members looked on these celebrations with suspicion and disapproval. They thought that the

Christmas celebrations bore too much of a resemblance to the old pagan rites of the winter solstice.

At the time of the Reformation, conservatives formed their own sects to cleanse and purify the church. One of these sects was the Puritans. In fact, it was a group of these same Puritans who emigrated to Plymouth Rock. After landing in America, they enacted a law, similar to one that had been in effect in England, that prohibited the celebration of Christmas. *Christmas had become illegal!* In the Massachusetts colony from 1659 until 1681, the celebration of Christmas was punishable with a fine.

But the widespread and deep-seated need for a celebration marking relief from the soul-withering darkness was not to be denied. Both the folk tradition and the Christian tradition survived and blended into the Christmas we know today—filled with quiet moments in which we can express our love for one another, boisterous moments of merrymaking, excessive feasting, and abundant gift giving, punctuated with rays of warmth and hope.

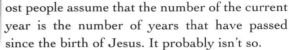

The Year

ost people assume that the number of the current year is the number of years that have passed since the birth of Jesus. It probably isn't so.

Sometime in the sixth century, a monk living in Rome, Dionysius Exiguus (Dennis the Little), separated history into the time before Jesus was born (B.C.) and the time after (A.D.). Before Dennis's time the year had been calculated from the date of the founding of Rome. Dennis set A.D. 1 as the year following Jesus' birth. But Dennis didn't count very well. We know from the Bible that Jesus was born in the reign of Herod. According to Dennis's own calculations, Herod died in 4 B.C. That is why it is likely that Jesus was born before 4 B.C.

The biblical description of the visit of the Magi to Herod's court makes no mention of Herod being ill or looking poorly. Most scholars assume that the visit of the Magi had to have taken place a few years before Herod died, and they assign Jesus' birth to the year 6 B.C. or 7 B.C.

Assuming that Jesus was born in either 6 B.C. or 7 B.C. might help to explain the miraculous Star of Bethlehem.

The Miraculous Star

That star atop Christmas trees celebrates what the Bible tells us is a miracle: the star of Bethlehem sent by the Lord to mark the birth of Jesus.

Was it a miracle or could there be another explanation?

The star isn't something that can be explained away as the sighting of a comet or meteor. In Jesus' time, one of the functions of pagan priests was to use their knowledge of the stars to advise common folk when to plant crops and when to harvest. There were many professional stargazers who were far too knowledgeable about comets and shooting stars to mistake one of those familiar objects for a miraculous phenomenon. Wise men would not have set out on the long journey of the Magi because of a comet or shooting star.

And, in the cold December nights around Bethlehem, it is unlikely that shepherds would be outside tending their flocks.

In fact, shepherds hardly ever tend their flocks at night, except during the spring lambing season. They would be more likely to be found inside local caves or in their tents. February 6th isn't exactly spring, but neither is it as wintry as December.

On February 6th in the year 6 B.C., an event occurred that might well have been regarded as a miraculous sign. Mars, Jupiter and Saturn lined up together in the sky and glowed with a startling brilliance, as if they were one celestial body. While the conjunction of two planets was not an especially rare event, the conjunction of the three occurs only once every 805 years, and astronomers would not have had prior knowledge of it. Even if they recognized it as a triple planetary juncture, its rarity might well have been regarded as special or thought to be a miraculous sign.

Those who believed that the stars controlled our destinies must have been overwhelmed by what they saw. Each planet involved in the conjunction has been assigned a role in men's affairs:

Jupiter—the King of the Gods
Saturn—the Protector of the Jews
Mars—the God of War.

This new "star" was seen in the constellation Pisces, which astrologers called the House of the Hebrews.

The astrologers "read" these signs to mean that a king would be born to the Hebrews and that his birth would lead to a war against established Roman rule. No wonder Herod grew fearful and sent out his soldiers to slay the newborn "King of the Jews." No wonder he asked the Magi to inform him when they located the Christ child.

The Star of Bethlehem

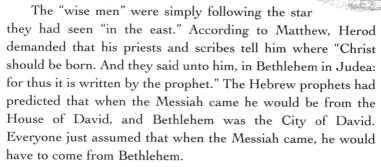

hy was it said that the Miraculous Star appeared over Bethlehem? When you look up to a star above the horizon it is difficult to say just what point on Earth it hovers over.

The "wise men" were simply following the star they had seen "in the east." According to Matthew, Herod demanded that his priests and scribes tell him where "Christ should be born. And they said unto him, in Bethlehem in Judea: for thus it is written by the prophet." The Hebrew prophets had predicted that when the Messiah came he would be from the House of David, and Bethlehem was the City of David. Everyone just assumed that when the Messiah came, he would have to come from Bethlehem.

Perhaps the star was just what the Bible tells us it was: a miraculous sign, hovering directly over the manger in Bethlehem, sent by God to announce glad tidings to the world.

The solemn star that shone so brightly in the east has become transformed into the much more cheerful and lively symbol that twinkles atop our trees today.

The Twelve Days of Christmas

hough December 25th had been assigned as Jesus' birthday, how did the "twelve days of Christmas" come to be?

The twelve days from December 25th to January 6th end in the Feast of the Epiphany, commemorating the visit of the wise men to Bethlehem. The celebration of the Feast of the Epiphany predates the celebration of Christmas. In early Christendom, before there ever was a Christmas Day, the Epiphany was regarded as the third most important holiday, after Easter and Pentecost. It had originated among eastern Christians as an alternative to pagan holidays celebrating the local river gods, and was intended to commemorate both the visit of the Magi and the baptism of Christ. After the western church declared December 25th Christmas Day, there were two important holidays in close proximity to one another, and some competition between them. Some Christians gave presents on Christmas Day while others gave presents on January 6th. Both traditions still exist.

Before Christianity, the period between the winter solstice

and the New Year had been a time of celebration in northern Germanic lands. The waning sun, visible only three or four hours each day, needed to be revived. A huge Yule log was cut from a giant oak and dragged from the forest to the hearth. There it was to burn or smolder to encourage the return of the sunlight. Originally the Yule festival lasted twelve nights. Kept indoors by the cold and darkness, the Norse thinned their herds, ate the meat and celebrated.

As the Roman legions marched northward, they learned of these celebrations. It occurred at the same time as their own winter solstice festival, Saturnalia, which in turn was followed by the New Year's festival of Calends. Gradually the two festivals became one long period of merrymaking and excess that usually lasted twelve days. These combined traditions were spread throughout the Roman empire, which included England, where many of our present traditions originated.

The church railed against the libertine partying but could not prevent the festivities, and so they did what they so often did before: they co-opted them by infusing them with Christian relevance. In 567, the Council of Bishops at Tours proclaimed the twelve days between Christmas and January 6th as sacred and festive.

From that time, Christian myths became associated with the holiday. The Magi of the Bible, the number unspecified, became "wise men"—though the original meaning of "magi" refers to priests or astrologers. In early Christian art there are sometimes two and sometimes four or more figures represented. But finally they were represented as three, probably because the Bible mentions three gifts: gold, frankincense and myrrh. Then they became "three kings of orient" and acquired names, Gaspar, Melchior and Balthazar, relating them to an Old Testament prophecy that kings bearing gifts would descend upon Israel.

In northern Europe, before the arrival of Christianity, they used to tell of the goddess Berchta who, accompanied by a dark dwarf, brought gifts at the time of the winter solstice. Today, in southern Europe, they tell the tale of La Befana, a small, gnarled woman at whose door the wise men stopped to ask directions. She noticed they carried gifts. Other people, each bearing a gift, also stopped to ask directions. Finally La

Befana decided to join them and took along a doll as her gift. But she arrived too late—Mary, Joseph and the baby had departed. It is said that to this day she wanders the earth on January 6th, stopping at each house to seek the Christ child, and leaving a small gift as she departs.

Why are there twelve days? Though there appears to be significance to the number twelve in religious literature—twelve tribes of Israel, Christ's twelve apostles, etc.—it is probably a coincidence. The twelve days are more likely to have arisen in an attempt to link the new holiday of December 25th with the more important "Old Christmas" day of the Feast of the Epiphany, January 6th.

Singing About the Twelve Days of Christmas

The song *The Twelve Days of Christmas* betrays its pagan origins. Songs that include counting—whether days or stars or toes—date, at least, to medieval folk songs.

The Twelve Days of Christmas has no religious content or references, other than the word "Christmas." It refers only to gifts. In its most popular version it refers to seven days of receiving birds (the "golden rings" of the fifth day refer to the bands around the necks of ring-necked pheasants), and five more days of people providing services or entertainment. Clearly it is a feast in progress, with birds to eat and birds to sing and entertain, along with people to serve. Earlier versions referred more directly to gifts of food.

$\mathcal{T}$welfth $\mathcal{N}$ight

he dozen days of the Christmas celebration ended in the biggest celebration of all, Twelfth Night.

In these more conservative times, the Twelfth Night is merely a signal to take down the tree and decorations. The demands of an industrialized society could no longer sanction nearly two weeks of drunken revelry, plus the time needed to recover from the wildest night of all, the Twelfth Night.

In medieval times, this final night was often referred to as the Feast of Fools. People dressed to disguise themselves. Men dressed as women, lords dressed as slaves and slaves might have dressed up as lords. Public order was suspended. Though gambling was illegal for most of the year, during this period it was allowed. Celebrants felt free to indulge themselves in rowdy sexual and wanton behavior.

This feasting and celebrating was presided over by the Lord of Misrule. Some trace his existence back to the

Mesopotamian celebration of Zagmuk in 2500 B.C. Mesopotamian law required that once each year the king be sacrificed to atone for the misdeeds of his people and to start the year afresh. And so, from the ranks of the condemned, the king would select a prisoner to be King for a Day. During his reign he would be obeyed as the king, and at day's end he would be sacrificed, meeting the requirements of the law.

In Roman times the sacrificial rites had been abandoned, but the tradition maintained for the Saturnalia festival. A slave or commoner was named overlord, and his wishes were obeyed as he presided over nobles who had given up their authority for the day.

Throughout the Middle Ages, the church gained authority by legitimizing the rule of various kings. An uneasy truce maintained a balance of power between church and state. Though the church preached against these pagan excesses, the kings did not wish to give them up. And so the holidays retained their revelry until the rise of Protestantism, with its drive to return the church to its simple roots in the teachings and lifestyle of Jesus.

Merry Christmas

Most religious holidays are somber and reverent. On other holidays people go to church and pray or do penance. Why is Christmas so *merry*?

The answer probably lies in the folk traditions that preceded the birth of Jesus. The winter solstice is the beginning of the new sun. For some, it was also the beginning of the New Year. For the Romans it was Saturnalia.

Saturnalia lasted from three to twelve days. Schools and courts were closed. There were feasts. Gambling was allowed. Streets were crowded with revelers singing and dancing. People would forget their place in society, dress up and wear masks. The masquerade permitted many to drink and party to excess anonymously. It was like a week of New Year's Eves.

This kind of celebrating was practiced for centuries. It became a part of the celebration of Christmas.

By the end of the Middle Ages, the "Christmas" celebrations of the nobility had reached such levels of extravagance and excess that the pious regarded them as too pagan.

St. Francis tried to restore the simplicity of the Nativity day and was partially successful. Centuries later, English Puritans, reacting to a continuation of the same celebratory excess, tried to outlaw Christmas celebrations of any kind.

But every year the darkness crept back. And as the light disappeared from the sky, people felt their spirits sinking. They watched for the sign that the light would be renewed and that the springtime would return. Their expressions of joy were natural and deeply heartfelt. They were eager to celebrate and feel good again. The folk tradition of wintertime merriment prevailed.

We still celebrate the New Year with excitement, and often with excess, to mark the opportunity to begin anew. And we celebrate the end of the darkness and the light of Christmas with the merriest and warmest of feelings, a blend of two deeply moving human emotions that had found their expression in St. Francis's piety and Roman revelry.

Foothills Congregational Church
Christmas Dinner

Wedon't usually celebrate with an Easter dinner or an Annunciation lunch that is the same from year to year. How did Christmas dinner become a tradition?

Saturn was the god of Agriculture, and the Roman Saturnalia festival featured lavish dining and excessive drinking.

Some of our present-day Christmas feasting may have its roots in these old Roman traditions. But there were practical considerations that may have been of greater importance.

Christmas comes after the harvest and, in many places, around the time of the first snowfall. In Scandinavia and

25

northern Germany, the cattle could no longer be put out to pasture. Rather than be left to go unfed, the herds would be thinned. There was a great quantity of meat for all. Having few ways to store and preserve the meat, people ate and drank before the meat would go to waste.

Traditional English roast beef probably descends from the practice of thinning the herds before the onset of the winter frost. Pigs were traditional Christmas fare in continental Europe. In England, the rich might hunt boar while the peasants slaughtered their pigs. Some English nobles had special royal dispensation to hunt swan, while the peasants pursued geese or grouse. In America, the wild birds that became the Christmas feast were more likely to be turkeys.

Christmas Dessert

One of the yearly specialties of Christmas dinner is dessert. In fact, through the ceturies each country has developed its own tradition of Christmas cakes.

The original English Christmas puddings—often made with dried fruits—betrayed their pagan origins by being baked with fortune-telling charms inside. If your slice contained a coin you would be rich in the coming year; a thimble, you would be an old maid; a button meant you would remain a bachelor; if you got a ring, you would be married. Plum pudding, so often sung about at Christmastime, has no plums in it. To plum meant to rise or swell up, and so a plum pudding was one that rose when

baked, or one that contained raisins that swelled up. Plum puddings were often made of meats and fruits that were at hand at that time of year, such as apples. Plums were rarely to be found in England in December.

Plum puddings were originally baked in oblong shapes to resemble the manger. Their latticework covers were meant to symbolize the hay racks. The Germanic peoples baked log-shaped loaves thought to have magic powers, especially if they contained the "dew of the Christmas night." These logs are reminiscent of their Yule log traditions. Stollen began with Bishop Heinrich von Naumberg in 1329, and were shaped to represent the Christ child in swaddling clothes. The French also baked cookies to resemble the Christ child, or, sometimes, to look like the Magi.

Today, Christmas remains a time for feasting. Even though supermarkets offer a greater variety of foods than were available to the celebrants of ancient times, most people ignore the wide selection and carry on the centuries-old traditions that make Christmas unique. Apparently we don't want to change our Christmas celebration. We want it the way it was when we were young. We want to hold on to the magic and the practices that make us feel so special on Christmas Day.

The Bringer of Gifts

W hy do we tell our children to go to bed so that Santa Claus can come and bring them gifts? Why don't we just give the children their gifts and admit they are from us?

A widespread belief in a supernatural bringer of gifts dates back thousands of years, although the person thought to be the gift giver differed from land to land and reflected local myths.

Saturn brought gifts to the Romans. The Scandinavians had the god Odin, who, in midwinter, rode on his eight-footed horse bringing gifts or, if you had been bad, bringing punishment. The British gift giver, Father Christmas, who probably originated during the time that the Norsemen settled in Britain, is derived from Odin. Odin usually left gifts of corn and fruit—the gifts of a good harvest—along with the promise that the earth would be fertile again. The French

Père Noel originally was the personification of the Christmas feast.

Both Father Christmas and Père Noel were actually substitutes for St. Nicholas, possibly the most widely beloved saint of all time. Stories about his generosity encouraged many to look to him for gifts and seek his aid. Though his "day" was set for December 6th, his legendary helpfulness caused many to associate him more and more with Christmas. After the Protestant Reformation, there was an effort to obliterate the worship of saints; all saints' holidays were banned. The British and French, while willing to give up St. Nicholas, were not willing to give up the traditions of their winter solstice holiday. So they reached into their folk myths and simply renamed the supernatural gift giver whose gift revealed whether you would be favored by the gods.

The Germanic peoples also had a tradition of a winter visitor; they looked to a goddess named Berchta who watched over children and visited them each December. She was accompanied by a dark dwarf who brought gifts to the good children and punished the bad ones.

As the Christmas holiday spread, the Christian tradition of love and the folk tradition of joy and hope fused, and the time was ripe for a new bringer of gifts, one who might better reflect this new blending of values.

St. Nicholas

St. Nicholas appears to have been the first mortal to be thought of as the bringer of gifts.

In the closing years of the fourth century he was the Bishop of Myra in Turkey. In his lifetime, there were many stories about his concern for the welfare of his parishioners and his generosity. Perhaps the tale told most often was of a father who did not have money enough to give any of his three daughters a dowry. In fact, the man was so poor that he might have had to sell his girls into slavery. Over the years, as each daughter came of age, Nicholas, cloaked by the darkness of night, tossed a bag of coins into the man's window.

Nicholas's gifts usually came as a complete surprise. After his death, the stories grew into the legend of a very kind and much-loved man who watched over people. Gradually his fame spread throughout the Mediterranean, and people celebrated his day on December 6th. The proximity of this day to Christmas Day caused the two holidays eventually to become intermingled.

St. Nicholas became so popular that many churches were named for him. He became the patron saint of Moscow and of Russia itself. Czars bore his name. "Nikita" means "little Nicholas." There used to be a saying among the Russians that "even if God dies, we still have St. Nicholas." By the thirteenth century, he had become the patron saint of children in Europe. And in England, there are more than twice as many churches dedicated to him as there are to England's own patron saint, St. George.

Apparently people wanted to feel that there were supernatural forces that looked after their welfare. They wanted to believe that someone might be kind and generous to them, particularly at this darkest time of year when they hoped for some prophetic sign to indicate their fortunes in the year to come. Would their gods judge them as being worthy? The visit from St. Nicholas is still regarded as a sign that we have been judged to have been good all year.

During the Reformation, when reformers wanted to discourage devotion to the Catholic saints, the Protestants suggested that the gifts came from the Christ child—in Martin Luther's Germany, the *Christ Kindl*. But the old myths were too powerful, and with time and usage the phrase became *Kris Kringle*—no longer a description of the Christ child, but, like Father Christmas and Père Noel, one more name for the man who today is also called Santa Claus.

Sinter Klaus

The name "Santa Claus" is derived from St. Nicholas. In Dutch, *Sinter Nicklaus* was shortened to *Sinter Klaus*, and in English mispronounced as *Santa Claus*.

How did we inherit Santa Claus from the Dutch?

The Dutch brought their Christmas traditions to their new-world colony of New Amsterdam. After the English conquered New Amsterdam and changed its name to New York, the Dutch eventually settled into a comfortable life in the new world and began to move away from many of their older traditions. *Sinter Klaus* became less prominent in their celebrations.

Some 150 years later, in 1809, an American of English descent wrote a book poking mild fun at the old Dutch settlers of New Amsterdam. It was Washington Irving's *Diedrich Knickerbocker's History of New York*, and included the following passage:

At this early period was instituted that pious ceremony, still religiously observed in all our ancient families of the right breed, of hanging up a stocking in the chimney on St.

Nicholas eve; which stocking is always found in the morning miraculously filled, for the good St. Nicholas has ever been a great giver of gifts, particularly to children.

Irving goes on to characterize St. Nicholas as a sort of patron of the Dutch settlement on Manhattan. Time and again he reappears in the book, as in this dream of Oloffe Van Kortlandt:

...and lo, the good St. Nicholas came riding over the tops of trees, in that selfsame wagon wherein he brings his yearly presents to children, and he descended...he lit his pipe by the fire, and sat himself down and smoked,...And when St. Nicholas had smoked his pipe, he twisted

it in his hat-band, and laying his finger beside his nose, gave the astonished Van Kortlandt a very significant look,...he returned over the tree-tops and disappeared.

Could a book have been so influential as to revive St. Nicholas Day celebrations? It might never have been, had Irving not created a fabulous hoax. On October 26, 1809, a notice was placed in the *New York Evening Post* that one Diedrich Knickerbocker, "a small elderly gentleman...not entirely in his right mind" had gone missing. The notice asked concerned citizens to notify the newspaper if they had any information. In those days, such a notice was sure to draw attention and become a major topic of conversation. Eleven days later a letter printed in the paper informed readers following this tale that a gentleman, who might fit the description, had been seen traveling north of the city. More news to discuss over an ale at the tavern.

Ten days more brought still one more newspaper notice, this time from Knickerbocker's landlord. He had entered his tenant's room and discovered a "curious kind of written book...in his own handwriting." As the rent had not been paid, he would have to dispose of the book to satisfy the debt. Good citizens speculated what the book might contain, and before speculation could die down, just twelve days later, the book was published and was an immediate bestseller. No book previously published in the United States had ever sold so well.

Washington Irving's promotional skills had created a publishing event! His letters to the newspaper had everyone talking. Though the practice of Christmas had been supressed among the English, St. Nicholas has long been an English favorite. It did not take much to bring him back to center stage. With the reference to hanging up one's stockings referred to as a practice among "families of the right breed," St. Nicholas and the celebration of his day were back in fashion.

Santa Claus

Y ou may call him St. Nicholas, St. Nick or Kris Kringle. Most Americans call him Santa Claus.

In 1822 the Reverend Clement Moore wrote *A Visit From St. Nicholas*, more popularly known as "The Night Before Christmas." He wrote it for his children, but did not wish to publish it because he feared it might damage his scholarly reputation as a lexicographer, poet and professor of Greek and Hebrew. A relative copied it down and showed it to a friend, who showed it to the editor of the *Troy Sentinel*, who published it, as an anonymous poem, in 1823. After many other publications of it, Moore finally claimed it as his own in 1837, but remained somewhat embarrassed by it right up to his death in 1863. It is

doubtful that he ever understood the significant contribution
he had made.

'Twas the night before Christmas, when all through the
    house
Not a creature was stirring, not even a mouse;
The stockings were hung by the chimney with care,
In hope that Saint Nicholas soon would be there;
The children were nestled all
    snug in their beds,
While visions of sugar plums
    danced in their heads;
And mamma in her kerchief
    and I in my cap
Had just settled our brains for
    a long winter's nap,
When out on the lawn there
    arose such a clatter,
I sprang from my bed to see
    what was the matter.

Away to the window I flew
    like a flash,

Tore open the shutters, and threw up the sash;
The moon on the breast of the new fallen snow,
Gave a lustre of midday to objects below;
When what to my wondering eyes should appear
But a miniature sleigh and eight tiny reindeer;
With a little old driver, so lively and quick
I knew in a moment, it must be St. Nick.

More rapid than eagles, his coursers they came,
And he whistled and shouted and called them by name;
"Now Dasher! now Dancer! now Prancer! now Vixen!
On, Comet! on, Cupid!, on Donder and Blitzen!
To the top of the porch! To the top of the wall!
Now, dash away, dash away, dash away, all!"

As dry leaves that before the wild hurricane fly,
When they meet with an obstacle, mount to the sky,
So up to the housetop the coursers they flew,
With the sleigh full of toys and Saint Nicholas too.
And then in a twinkling, I heard on the roof
The prancing and pawing of each little hoof.
As I drew in my head and was turning around

Down the chimney Saint Nicholas came with a bound.

Following Irving's lead, Moore described Santa quite
vividly:

He was dressed all in fur, from his head to his foot,
And his clothes were all tarnished with ashes and soot;
A bundle of toys he had flung on his back,
And he looked like a peddler just opening his pack.
His eyes—how they twinkled! His dimples how merry!
His cheeks were like roses, his nose like a cherry!
His droll little mouth was drawn up like a bow,
And the beard of his chin was as white as the snow,
The stump of a pipe he held tight in his teeth,
And the smoke it encircled his head like a wreath;
He had a broad face and a round little belly
That shook when he laughed like a bowl full of jelly.
He was chubby and plump, a right jolly old elf
And I laughed when I saw him, in spite of myself.

Was Santa an "elf" so that he could fit into the chimney?
Or was this a carryover of much earlier European traditions

that often described the gift giver as a dwarf or as having a dwarf helper?

> A wink of his eye and a twist of his head
> Soon gave me to know I had nothing to dread.
> He spoke not a word, but went straight to his work,
> And filled all the stockings; then turned with a jerk,
> And laying his finger aside of his nose,
> And giving a nod, up the chimney he rose,

Almost the same gesture as reported by Irving in Van Kortlandt's dream!

> He sprang to his sleigh, to his team gave a whistle
> And away they all flew like the down of a thistle;
> But I heard him exclaim, ere he drove out of sight,
> "Happy Christmas to all, and to all a good night!"

The spread of Moore's poem through the first half of the nineteenth century coincided with the immigration of a large body of Germans to the U.S. eastern farm country. Unlike the English Protestants, the Germans had not abandoned their

Christmas festivities. It was celebrated as a family holiday with special emphasis on the children. Moore's poem, written for his children, fit right in with German Christmas trees, handmade toys and decorations and carol singing. If Irving had helped bring the English back to celebrating Christmas, Moore and the Germans helped to spread the merry-making for everyone to enjoy.

That Santa Claus Look

We think of Santa as a full-grown man, red-cheeked and chubby. We would probably agree on just what he looks like. How did we come to this agreement?

In Moore's poem *A Visit From St. Nicholas,* not only is Santa an elf, but he drives "a miniature sleigh with eight tiny reindeer." The poem grew in popularity over the years. Moore himself made no money from his delightful creation, but publishers were quick to capitalize on its commercial possibilities, bringing out new and more lavish editions, competing with one another to attract sales. In 1863, one publisher hired the illustrator Thomas Nast to dress up his latest edition. Nast, who in later years was to gain fame as an extraordinarily effective political cartoonist, drew Santa from Moore's description. Nast made Santa into a full-sized "Dutch uncle." In *The Christmas Almanack,* the authors believe that Moore's description was based on the caretaker of their house, Jan Duyckinck, who they say was "fat,… jolly,…bewhiskered…known for the old pipe he kept clenched in his teeth."

In old illustrations and the figurines sold at craft shows, one can see very different images of Christmastime gift givers. Father Christmas may be depicted as tall and thin, with a long, stern face, often without a beard. St. Nicholas is frequently shown as a tall, hooded figure, more like a monk than the fur-trimmed, red-suited Santa of our childhood. It is to Washington Irving, Clement Moore and Thomas Nast that Santa owes his present form, his North Pole home, his workshop full of elves and his reindeer.

The final, full color transformation of Santa into the "ho ho ho," red-cheeked figure most familiar to our eyes may be traced to a series of Coca-Cola ads drawn by Haddon Sundblom during the 1920s.

The Reindeer

Reindeer? What a strange way to travel! Reindeer, and whatever traditions exist about them, obviously come from northern climes. For centuries reindeer have been used to pull sleds in Lapland. But the connection between Santa and the reindeer is more modern. Until the nineteenth century St. Nicholas was usually depicted as riding on a donkey or a horse or sometimes in a chariot.

It was Clement Moore who gave Santa his eight reindeer: Dasher, Dancer, Prancer and Vixen, Comet, Cupid, Donder and Blitzen. In their names we hear the echoes of the two goats, Gnasher and Cracker, who pulled the cart for Thor, the Norse thunder god.

What about Rudolph? He isn't mentioned at all! Rudolph is actually a much later addition. Rudolph was created in 1939 by an advertising copywriter, Robert May, for Montgomery

Ward's department store. Unfortunately, Rudolph did not make much of a splash at the time. However, in 1946, Wards wanted something for their in-store Santa Claus to hand out to children, so they revived and promoted the Rudolph story. Early the following year songwriter Johnny Marks saw a write-up about Rudolph in a magazine and wrote the now-famous song *Rudolph the Red-Nosed Reindeer*. It was popularized by the singing cowboy, Gene Autry, whose recording was released in 1949.

So it was the business world that not only gave us that Santa Claus look, but also gave us "the most famous reindeer of them all." As the song predicted, Rudolph appears to have become more closely associated with Christmas than any of the other reindeer.

Christmas Presents

Why do we give and receive gifts on a religious holiday? There isn't any other Christian holiday when gifts are exchanged. Children's Easter baskets don't quite fit the same level of gift giving.

The folk tradition of giving gifts at the winter solstice goes back to a time before the birth of Jesus. The Norse god Odin came through the snow to bring gifts of fruit and corn to signify the coming of spring. Evergreens were also highly prized gifts because they mysteriously refused to die even in the depths of winter when all other trees had shed their leaves. These were not personal gifts, however, but merely the symbols of hope for the future.

The Romans had two gift-giving holidays, both in December. Saturnalia, celebrated on the day of the winter solstice, was an occasion for the rich to give gifts to the poor and for the poor to give gifts of evergreens or candles. Green branches were a symbol of life and the Italian countryside provided olive, bay leaf and myrtle boughs at that time of year.

Candles symbolized that the light that nurtured the earth would return.

Saturnalia was quickly followed by Calends, the Roman New Year, from which we get our word *calendar*. The New Year was a time of prophecies and omens. Gifts were symbols of the giver's wishes for the new year. Sweets, such as dates, figs, honey, cakes or fruit, were given to wish someone good times; gold- or silver-colored objects, such as gilded nuts, were to wish someone wealth in their future. Calends gifts were personal gifts. They revealed whether others thought you were worthwhile.

Eventually, the two holidays joined into one long celebration of feasting and merriment. Though Christianity triumphed, the Romans, who had a history of tolerating many religions, simply continued their winter festivities and included Christmas in their merrymaking.

Gifts became elaborate, celebrations became excessive. The early Christian church frowned on both as throwbacks to paganism and there was an attempt to ban gift giving. Once again, folk customs were too strong to be overcome. People wanted to receive gifts because gifts helped them feel that someone cared about them. People wanted to give gifts to those they cared about. By the twelfth century, the custom of gift giving had become so ingrained that the church muted its opposition and began to speak of gift giving as a reflection of the gifts given by the Magi to the Christ child.

Christmas Toys

oday, the most popular Christmas gifts are toys. In Europe, during the Middle Ages, St. Nicholas had become the patron saint of children. As his December 6th holiday merged with Christmas, and as he became the acknowledged bringer of gifts, it was only natural for Christmas to become more of a children's celebration.

The Christmas emphasis on giving toys to children originated in Germanic lands. There, Christmas had become more of a family holiday instead of one associated with giving gifts to friends, which had been the Roman Saturnalia tradition. Originally the Germans made wooden toys to give to their children. When the holiday spread to the lands of the Franks, the

French gave more emphasis to making and giving dolls.

Today, all kinds of toys, dolls and games are given to the delight of children everywhere.

Christmas Stockings

What did you find in your Christmas stocking? Today, your stocking may hold the smaller gifts. But years ago, the stocking was everything. On wet or snowy days children were told to leave their shoes on the hearth to dry out. When St. Nicholas made one of his unexpected visits, whether it was snowy or not, he would leave presents in their shoes.

No one knows just when stockings replaced shoes as the receptacles for Santa's gifts. Perhaps shoes were too wet or too small. As dolls and carved toys became prominent Christmas gifts, larger receptacles were necessary. In the twentieth century, commercial interests began to offer stockings especially made for the occasion. Though Christmas stockings have become almost universal, there were other traditions, some of which are still practiced today.

In Germany there was a tradition of the gifts being attached to the limbs of the tree. Our current practice of leaving gifts under the tree may have evolved from this German tradition. In lands where the bringer of gifts is thought to be the Christ child, gifts are often left next to the crèche.

Though some measure of extravagance has been associated with December gift giving since the time of the Romans, it was the commercially minded Victorians who turned Christmas into the gift bonanza we know today. The symbolism of gifts of green or gold and the mementos of light gave way to status gifts and the anxiety that one did not give enough.

In 1994, the average American family spent over $430 on Christmas gifts. Consumerism has given the Christmas spirit a sharp nudge and today the presents are often piled so high that neither the stocking nor the tree can contain them.

Trees

Today we chop down or buy a tree, carry it home, set it up in a stand, decorate it and place our presents underneath it. It wouldn't seem like Christmas without a tree. How did trees become so important in our celebration of Christmas?

Trees were originally given as New Year's gifts. And, like other New Year's gifts, trees had symbolic significance. Originally, almond, hawthorn, blackthorn and other trees with bright, small blossoms were kept indoors and their blossoms forced, in hopes that they would appear by the New Year. If they did, it was regarded as a good omen for the crops in the coming year. But forcing blossoms was a chancy business, and rather than tempt

fate, many turned to evergreen trees, especially those that bore fruit at the New Year.

The evergreen was a great mystery. Why should it remain green and, as in the case of the holly, even bear fruit, in a season when all other types of trees seemed to die? People thought evergreens had magical powers and would ward off evil spirits. Evergreens were especially popular in Germanic lands. where they were plentiful.

The oak was sacred to the Celtic Druids. At the winter solstice, they decorated oaks with candles and apples painted gold. In one legend, on an eighth-century Christmas Eve/solstice night, St. Boniface chopped down a huge oak that had been used for human sacrifice and, pointing to a young fir that had survived the crash of the oak, told the assembled barbarians that this "young child in the forest" should be their holy tree.

Trees, like oaks which outlive man by hundreds of years, or evergreens which never seem to wither, were believed to contain a mysterious life force. They became central features of the rites celebrated on the darkest day of winter, when the life force seemed most vulnerable.

O Christmas Tree

A tree designated as a *Christmas* tree made its first appearance in the late sixteenth century. It was merely the latest in a long line of mystical or sacred trees that held special significance in popular folklore.

In the earliest description of a *Christmas* tree, that heritage is clear. In a fragment from a travel diary dated 1605, an unidentified visitor to Strasbourg, Germany, describes tree decorations that include apples (from the Tree of Life?), paper roses (from solstice celebrations?), sweets, wafer-like cookies (to wish for good times in the coming year?) and golden spangles (to wish for riches?).

When England's Queen Victoria married Germany's Prince Albert, the Christmas tree became quite central to the holiday in the British Isles. It was a time of Victorian commercialism, and of a growing middle class eager for ways to display their new wealth. The tree provided an opportunity to sell more goods to the public and was vigorously promoted.

British and European trees were only two feet high and sat on tabletops. Tall trees were too precious to be cut down as adornments. Christmas trees had not been officially sanctioned by the church and many regarded them as frivolous. In fact, in Germany, where the use of evergreens in winter celebrations began, there was a ban on cutting down large trees for Christmas.

German immigrants brought the Christmas tree tradition to America. The rich natural resources of the North American continent combined with something in the American personality and gave rise to the floor-to-ceiling trees so common today. In 1995 Americans bought more than thirty-three million real trees. More than thirty-six million artificial trees were also on display.

Decorating the Tree

Each year, you probably bring out the same boxes of glass and metal ornaments to decorate the tree, but the earliest known tree decorations were edibles.

Up until the latter portion of the nineteenth century, candies, sweets, cookies and fruits adorned the tree. Gradually the cookies and sweets were made in decorative shapes and colors. Large cookies were made in the shapes of soldiers, dolls and animals. Nuts were painted gold to add a bright glow and were the forerunners of glistening balls.

Sparkling, colored paper cones filled with tiny candies were hung from the tree. Candy makers offered their wares strung together in garlands, ready for the tree. With so many goodies, Christmas trees were often called "sugar trees." When the tree was taken down on Twelth Night it was an occasion for feasting on the tree decorations. Homemade paper ornaments, cut in the shapes of spring flowers or animals, were also quite popular.

In the 1870s, as the Victorian business ethic took hold, the first commercially made ornaments appeared in Germany. These ornaments simply took the shapes that people were already making for themselves at home and upgraded the materials so that they might be worth buying and keeping. The earliest commercially sold ornaments were made of cardboard, embossed with silver and gold, and shaped like the animals and fish that had previously been made from cookie dough or cut from paper. Three-dimensional ornaments were made to be purchased and assembled at home. By the end of the decade tinsel icicles were coming into use.

The first blown-glass ornaments came from Lauscha, Germany, in the 1880s. They were little more than glass bubbles in various colors. Soon the glass was being blown into molds to make glass pine cones or fruits. This was a cottage industry and whole families were involved in their manufacture. The father would heat one end of a glass rod to a specific melting point, insert it into a mold and blow the other end to make the glass fill the mold. After it cooled, someone would swirl a silver nitrate solution inside the ornament to make it sparkle. Other family members would paint parts of the ornament, add the caps and pack them for shipment.

It is curious that so few of these ornaments depicted religious figures. Dolls, heads, clowns, icicles, Santas, fish and animals were among the most prominent ornaments vigorously promoted by F.W. Woolworth stores in the United States in the 1890s. Christmas was once more wriggling free of its Christian trappings and asserting its boisterous folk tradition. Germany had become the world center of glass ornament production. Today, these antique glass ornaments are expensive, eagerly sought-after collectibles.

The use of electric tree lights began in 1882 with Edward Johnson, an associate of Thomas Edison, who put them on his own tree. Before that, candles were widely used.

Candles

he Christmas candle in the window touches most travelers and gives them an inner glow. Is there anything as heartwarming as a light in the window after walking a long dark road? Candles aroused this feeling long before there was a Christmas.

No winter solstice celebration would have been imagined without candles. They were the symbols of the return of the sun and, ultimately, the springtime, the harvest and the full larder.

Candles were prominent features of the Roman Saturnalia celebrations. They were more expensive to use than oil lamps and had become major gift items as well as festival decorations. In those days, candles were often made of beeswax and were costly gifts, usually exchanged by wealthy families. Candles declined in significance as cheaper tallow candles became available.

Hundreds of years later, as church mythology enveloped the holiday, candles were said to represent a welcome to the

Christ child on his journey to Nazareth. At Christmastime, candles were to be seen glowing in windows across the countryside. Martin Luther said they were a reflection of the starry heavens from which Jesus had come.

Though the church usually fought against continuing any form of pagan symbolism, the church powers were, in this case, merely bowing to the inevitable. Candles had always represented warmth and home in the ominous dark of winter, and their light at the end of the road symbolized hope for the sunny spring to come, and on a more personal level, the hope for a brighter future.

Decorating the House

We like to think of the holly wreaths on our doors and ivy garlands that may encircle our windows as symbols of Christmas. But using evergreens to decorate the house is much older than Christmas itself.

The earliest available reports of decorating the house are from Roman times. As Saturnalia and Calends joined together into a week-long festival, a carnival atmosphere spread throughout the community. People decorated their doorways with green branches and boughs. They kept their homes ablaze with lights.

Evergreens were the most popular decorations. Those that bore winter fruit, such as holly and mistletoe, were not merely prized decorations, but were regarded as sacred representations of the mysterious life force. Romans gave evergreen branches to one another symbolizing the wish for a verdant spring to come. Many twined the branches into garlands and into wreaths.

Poinsettias are a recent addition to Christmas decorations. They are from Mexico, where they are known as the "flower of the holy night." Legend tells of a poor Mexican boy who had no gift for the Christ child. He prayed for a present and the plant magically appeared. The flowers get their English name from the U.S. ambassador to Mexico of the late 1800s, Dr. Joel Poinsett, who helped popularize them in the United States.

Our Christmas garlands and wreaths, the lights in our windows and the poinsettias on our tables have a venerable tradition of bringing good cheer into the dark days of winter.

Mistletoe

istletoe is a parasite that grows in the high branches of trees. It never touches the earth. It must have been a profound source of mystery to the ancients to explain how something could grow without the nurturance of the soil. And not only grow, but bloom in winter as well! Clearly the gods must have intervened.

According to Norse myth, when Frigga gave birth to Baldur, the sun god, she was so fearful for his future that she traveled the earth and exacted a promise from every creature, and from every rock and stream and tree, that they would bring no harm to her son. But the mistletoe was so lowly that she overlooked it. Loki, the god of mischief, was aware of this omission. He contrived to have someone shoot Baldur with an arrow made of mistletoe. The death of Baldur represents the end of sunlight in December. Frigga, who was also the goddess of love, restored her son to life and her tears turned to white berries on the mistletoe arrow shaft (why mistletoe berries bloom in winter). In her jubilation over having saved her son, she declared that the mistletoe would forever after be capable of bringing only love to the world. All who came beneath it should embrace and feel kindness for one another. Mistletoe's association with restoring life to the sun god also led to its use for a variety of illnesses. Its name, in the Celtic tongue, meant "heal all."

The practice of hanging mistletoe over doorways and kissing those who passed beneath can be traced back to the Druids. The Celts, the Norse and the Druids promoted mistletoe in England. Though the church never gave mistletoe official status, its magical powers to create harmony and amity became the stuff of folk legend. It was rumored that if enemies met beneath it, they would lay down their weapons.

Mistletoe has no specific association with Christmas. Its inclusion among the holly and the evergreens is due to its winter fruit, its association with love and amity and its general magical powers. Mistletoe may originally have been associated with the New Year, when a variety of magical tools were used to assure that the coming year would be filled with prosperity and happiness.

Christmas Bells

The bells on Christmas Day are the same bells rung on other days to call the congregation to prayer. But bells have a history, far removed from quiet prayer, as noisemakers with a very special purpose. The winter solstice was a time to consult omens to predict a person's fortunes for the coming year. This was a very serious business. People did not consult the omens lightly or unprepared. Before consultation began they wanted to drive the evil spirits away. Evil spirits were driven out by noise. There were pagan traditions of horn- and whistle-blowing, beating drums, and ringing bells. In later times people set off firecrackers and guns as well as other fireworks to disturb and dislodge the evil around them.

The British pull "crackers" at the Christmas dinner table. These cardboard and paper containers burst open with a loud firecracker-like pop and usually contain candy (sweets), a paper hat (masquerade) and a little gift (worthiness).

Many of these noise-making traditions have been sanitized of their pagan purposes and passed on to us as practices suited to more Christian celebrations. While most whistle- and horn-blowing has been relegated to New Year's Eve, bells are rung on both occasions.

Bells were also used year round to announce events. By the sixth century they were used to announce Jesus' birthday. Throughout the Middle Ages they remained in use both to announce news and to thwart evil.

Our Christmas bells both announce the good tidings and reassure us that we need not fear the presence of evil. They ring out the "good news"—the original meaning of the Old English word *gospels*.

The Nativity Crèche

erhaps we are not surprised to learn that many
Christmas practices date from a time before Christ's
birth. And it may be perfectly logical that many other
practices are far more modern. But surely there is good reason
to think that the familiar Nativity scene comes down to us
from the actual event of Jesus' birth, even though it doesn't
make its first appearance for more than one thousand years.

Around A.D. 1000, cribs of gold and silver decorated with
precious stones could be found in churches throughout the
Roman empire. In 1224, St. Francis of Assisi, wanting to
remind people of the solemn religious meaning of the holiday,
set up a living crèche, based on the description in the Bible.
But it wasn't exactly the same as described in the Bible. St.
Francis's love of animals prompted him to add the ox, ass and
sheep, which are not mentioned in the biblical passages. It is
St. Francis's conception of the manger that we see so frequently today.

St. Francis kept his crèche as humble as possible. The display became quite famous and widely imitated. But the folk spirit of the holiday did not lend itself to Franciscan simplicity. Eventually pagan elaboration crept into the representation of the Nativity scene. Before long, nobles and kings hired famous artists to design their crèche scenes. The Magi became more majestic. The simplicity that St. Francis sought was lost again.

Today one can find both simple and elaborate crèche scenes. Perhaps each has something to tell us about the spirit of the holiday.

Singing Carols

or a month before Christmas Day some people complain that all they hear are carols. Yet once there were no carols sung because the church sought to abolish them and promote the singing of Latin hymns instead.

The word *carol* originally meant "dance music." It was joyous music and when it had words, they were in the everyday language of the people. Carols were not originally connected to Christmas, which was dominated by hymn singing.

By the thirteenth century, St. Francis longed for a more human, emotional appeal to the holiday. He tried to incorporate lay folk music into his Christmas celebrations. One of his disciples, Jacopone da Todi, wrote the first Christmas songs. In them, he attempted to describe the holiday as one of family joys and traditional family values, expressed in plain, everyday language. As his Franciscan brethren preached throughout Italy, they also taught these new Christmas songs.

During medieval times the poor went from door to door, cup in hand, and asked for a cup of hot wassail. The request was often made in rhyme. Hence "wassailing" came to refer to the same activity as "caroling." Once again the folk traditions associated with the winter holiday persisted. Joyous songs in the everyday language of the people had become firmly attached to the holiday celebration.

Many of the Christmas carols most familiar to us were written in Europe in the eighteenth century. *Joy to the World* dates from 1719, *Hark! The Herald Angels Sing* from 1739, and *O Come All Ye Faithful* from 1751. Then carols began to go out of style.

What may be the most popular carol of all, *Silent Night* was written as a last-minute replacement, on Christmas Eve, in 1818, in Obendorf, Germany. The organ had broken down and Father Josef Mohr, an assistant priest, needed something for the choir to sing to the only available accompaniment—a guitar!

He quickly jotted down the poem that is now famous all over the world. Then he asked his friend Franz Gruber to set it to music. The carol passed from hand to hand and thirty years later this lovely carol was sung throughout Europe—but without any knowledge of who had written it. Gruber stepped forward to claim co-authorship (Mohr was dead), but it took many years for either music authorities or church authorities to acknowledge him as the composer.

The Victorian period, with German-born Prince Albert's emphasis on Christmas, and the popularity of Charles Dickens's *A Christmas Carol*, brought a revival of interest in Christmas carols—first in England and then very emphatically in the United States, with its large immigrant German population. *It Came Upon a Midnight Clear* first appeared in 1849 in Massachusetts, *We Three Kings of Orient Are* came from Williamsport, Pennsylvania, in 1857, and *O Little Town of Bethlehem* from Philadelphia in 1868.

By the mid-nineteenth century the church had accepted carols as part of the Christmas celebration. Today, carols have become so familiar that they may seem old-fashioned to some. Younger people have turned to jazz carols and carols with a rock beat. These new rhythms might strike some as sacrilegious, but aren't they just what carols were originally intended to be: an expression of faith in everyday language and popular song?

Christmas Songs

If Christmas carols come from a tradition of popularizing the music of Christmas, then Christmas songs seem a natural extension of that tradition in more modern dress. Often they avoid the strictly religious aspect of Christmas, but their message usually reflects the pre-Christian traditional themes of the winter festival.

Some modern songs speak of home and hearth and the love of family that can be found there. Other lyrics reflect a desire for the reassurance that those forces that are greater than man will be beneficial and bring good cheer. The third common Christmas song theme refers to the joys of winter, the relaxation and fun of this celebratory season.

The number-one Christmas record, Bing Crosby's recording of Irving Berlin's *White Christmas*, has sold thirty million copies since its release in 1942. No other record in history had ever sold more than eight million copies. Released during another time of darkness, World War II, it brought the same reassurance of the triumph of human values that our ancestors had sought in the darkest days of the pre-Christian era. These sentiments are echoed in another perennial, *The Christmas Song,* which starts with "Chestnuts roasting on an open fire," as well as in songs such as *I'll Be Home for Christmas.*

All Christmas songs have a commercial motive. The most successful ones either find the merry mood, the underlying human need for love and home, or the reassurance gained from approval by supernatural forces.

The tale of *Rudolph, the Red-Nosed Reindeer* is the old moral fable of the outcast or failure being chosen or rewarded by the supernatural, in this case, Santa Claus himself. There is a more direct statement of this in *Santa Claus Is Coming to Town*: "You better watch out, you better not cry,..." After Gene Autry had made a hit of "Rudolph," he moved on to a different, but no less magical fable with *Frosty the Snowman* in 1951. Autry had his first big Christmas hit in 1946 with *Here Comes Santa Claus.*

What may be the most popular of all Christmas songs, *Jingle Bells,* never refers to Christmas in its lyrics. Like *Winter*

Wonderland, it is about wintertime and the snow, but it captures the underlying joyous holiday mood perfectly with its jaunty melody and jingling words. It dates to 1857 and the Victorian revival.

Each year we sing the oft-told tales of home and hearth, of redemption and divine intervention, and, finally, of the fun of the winter season. It's all as much a part of a modern Christmas as the solemnity surrounding the birth of Jesus.

Christmas Cards

These days, when we send out so many cards, it may be difficult to imagine that Christmas cards were originally handmade. In fact, some of the first commercial Christmas cards were printed without color so that the buyer could add color and still send a "hand made" card.

The first commercially illustrated Christmas card dates from 1843 and was made in England shortly after the introduction of low-cost printing methods. England already had seen Valentine's and New Year's cards, but these were the first for Christmas. Commissioned by Sir Henry Cole and drawn by John Calcott Horsley, the first Christmas card had three panels: the left one was entitled "Feeding the Hungry," the right one "Clothing the Naked," and the middle one depicted a family at table, with everyone raising their glasses to the reader of the card. The Victorian era focused rather strongly on Christmas. Charles Dickens wrote *A Christmas Carol* in the 1880s, and it was at this time that a moneyed middle class—a merchant class—began to emerge in England. They liked having new ways in which they could display their wealth and compete with one another.

The popularity and widespread use of Christmas cards in England was no doubt the result of both low-cost printing and the introduction of the penny post in the 1840s. Not only was it no longer necessary to sit at home and laboriously make scores of cards, but now the post would deliver them for very little money. Before this, postage cost was based on the number of pages and the distance traveled and was paid by the recipient! The combination of ready-made cards and an inexpensive mode of delivery proved irresistible and the craze had begun.

Today, it is estimated that in the United States alone, 2.7 billion cards are sent at Christmastime, with the average household receiving twenty-eight cards.

Where Does Christmas Come From?

Our Christmas practices have many ancestors. St. Nicholas came from Turkey, Santa Claus from Holland, the tree from Germany, our carols from England, poinsettias from Mexico and candles and the spirit of merriment from the Romans. Reindeer came from the Lapps and mistletoe from the Norse. There are contributions from pagan Druids and pious monks. And perhaps that is how it should be.

Christmas may have come from many lands. Christmas may be a happy blend of folk traditions and Christian traditions. Yet everywhere it is celebrated, it reflects the same poignant human yearnings for love and for a reason to hope.

Indeed it is the light of the world; the hearth in the cold of winter, and the beacon in the darkness.

So finally, where *does* Christmas come from?

It comes from our hearts.

Bibliography and Suggestions for Further Reading

Ashdown, Dulcie M., ed. *Christmas Past: A Selection from Victorian Magazines*. London: Elm Tree Books, 1976.

Barnett, James H. *The American Christmas*. New York: Macmillan, 1954.

Barth, Edna. *Holly, Reindeer and Colored Lights*. New York: Seabury Press, 1971.

Book of Christmas, The. Pleasantville, New York: Reader's Digest, 1973.

Coffin, Tristram P. *The Illustrated Book of Christmas Folklore*. New York: Seabury Press, 1973.

Ebon, Martin. *Saint Nicholas: Life and Legend*. New York: Harper & Row, 1975.

Emrich, Duncan. "A Certain Nicholas of Patara," *American Heritage Magazine*, December 1960.

Daniel, J. *The Christmas Tree*. Philadelphia: Chilton, 1960.

Del Re, Gerard & Patricia. *The Christmas Almanack.*
Garden City, N.Y.: Doubleday & Co., 1979.

Forbes, William J. "The Story of Christmas Trees" in *The Illustrated London News*, Christmas 1958.

Godden, Rumer. "The History of Christmas" in *The Book of Christmas*. Pleasantville, N.Y.: Reader's Digest, 1973.

International Book of Christmas Carols. Englewood Cliffs, N.J.: Prentice Hall Inc., 1963.

Irving, Washington. *Diedrich Knickerbocker's History of New York*. New York: Heritage Press, 1940.

Jones, E. Willis. *The Santa Claus Book*. New York: Walker & Co., 1976.

Life Book of Christmas, The. New York: Time Inc., 1963.

Merck, Robert M. *Deck the Halls*. New York: Abbeville Press, 1992.

Metcalf, Edna. *The Trees of Christmas.* New York: Abingdon Press, 1969.

Mitchell, Glenn. "Everything You Always Wanted to Know About Christmas" in *American Way* magazine, December 1, 1993.

Moore, Clement C. *The Night Before Christmas.* New York: Weathervane Books, 1976.

Muir, Frank. *Christmas Customs and Traditions*. New York: Taplinger Publishing Co. Inc., 1977.

Paine, Albert B. *Thomas Nast: His Period and His Pictures*. Reprint of the 1904 edition, Princeton, N.J.: Pyne Press, 1974.

Sansom, William. *A Book of Christmas*. New York, Toronto: McGraw Hill Book Co., 1968.

Shoemakers, Alfred L. "Christmas in Pennsylvania: A Folk Cultural Study." Kutztown, PA.: Pennsylvania Folklife Society, 1959.

Snyder, Philip. *December 25th. The Joys of Christmas Past*. New York: Dodd, Mead & Co., 1985.

Snyder, Philip. *The Christmas Tree Book*. New York: Viking Press, 1976.

Stevens, Patricia Bunning. *Merry Christmas—A History of the Holiday*. New York: Macmillan, 1970.

A BOOK FOR ANY SEASON AND ANY REASON...

__THE BOOK OF DAYS by Guen Sublette 0-399-51976-9/$12.00
A collection of fascinating facts, history and trivia about celebrations—from
the totally traditional to the completely obscure.

__WOMEN WHO JOKE TOO MUCH compiled by Silver Rose
0-399-52154-2/$9.00
A lively collection of quotes from the world's funniest women on every
important subject from dating to divorce, pets to politics.

__THE BOOK OF THANKSGIVING by Paul Dickson 0-399-52163-1/$9.00
A fully-illustrated celebration of the traditions and festivities surrounding
the most popular holiday in America.

__ETHEL BURKE'S WHAT I HATE ABOUT CHRISTMAS
by Ed Strnad, writing as Ethel Burke   0-399-52165-8/$8.00
Ethel Burke shares her thoughts on what makes Christmas irritating and
exasperating, and yet still the most charming of holidays.

__SNOW by Lisbeth Mark and Babs Lefrak   0-399-52166-6/$10.00
A celebration of snow, a unique beautiful gift.

Payable in U.S. funds. No cash orders accepted. Postage & handling: $1.75 for one book, 75¢ for each additional. Maximum postage $5.50. Prices, postage and handling charges may change without notice. Visa, Amex, MasterCard call 1-800-788-6262, ext. 1, refer to ad # 684a

| **Or, check above books** | **Bill my:** ☐ Visa   ☐   MasterCard ☐ Amex expires ____ |
| **and send this order form to** Card#_____ |
| The Berkley Publishing Group | |
| 390 Murray Hill Pkwy., Dept. B   Signature_____ ($15 minimum) |
| East Rutherford, NJ 07073 | |
| Please allow 6 weeks for delivery. **Or enclosed is my:** ☐ check ☐ money order |

Name_____	Book Total	$_____
Address_____	Postage & Handling	$_____
City_____	Applicable Sales Tax	$_____
	(NY, NJ, PA, CA, GST Can.)	
State/ZIP_____	Total Amount Due	$_____